Navigating the Waters

poems by

Sandy Longley

Finishing Line Press
Georgetown, Kentucky

Navigating the Waters

Copyright © 2016 by Sandy Longley
ISBN 978-1-63534-074-7 First Edition
All rights reserved under International and Pan-American Copyright Conventions. No part of this book may be reproduced in any manner whatsoever without written permission from the publisher, except in the case of brief quotations embodied in critical articles and reviews.

ACKNOWLEDGMENTS

These poems have appeared in the following publications:

Down in the Dirt,: "Metamorphosis"
Mudfish: "Derma Blues"
Naugatuck River Review: "The Crossing"
New Millennium Writings: "Early Warning Signs"
Nimrod International Journal: "Sky Watch," " What We Know"
Passager: "Rivers Rising"
Southword Journal: "Solace at the P.O.," "Stand Back"
Spillway: "Argonauta," "More than we ask for, more than we know," "When a Black Bear Came to Truro"
The Storyteller: "Metamorphosis"

Publisher: Leah Maines

Editor: Christen Kincaid

Cover Art: Linda Turoczi

Author Photo: Rob Longley

Cover Design: Elizabeth Maines

Printed in the USA on acid-free paper.
Order online: www.finishinglinepress.com
       also available on amazon.com

Author inquiries and mail orders:
Finishing Line Press
P. O. Box 1626
Georgetown, Kentucky 40324
U. S. A.

Table of Contents

Stand Back 1
Rivers Rising 2
The Crossing 3
Sometimes 5
Nocturne, in Red and Black 6
Minor Deviations 8
What We Know 9
Argonauta 10
Departures 11
Metamorphosis 12
Fifteen 13
Flying Light 14
Arrhythmia 15
Derma Blues 16
Solace at the P.O. 17
Alchemy 18
Reverie, Morning 20
Here on Earth 21
Sky Watch 23
for Dorothy Wordsworth 24
Early Warning Signs 25
Musa Nana 26
Sappho Sings to the Syrian Migrants on Lesbos ... 27
When a Black Bear Came to Truro 28
More than we ask for, more than we know 29

*"How can one learn to live through the ebb tides of one's existence?
How can one learn to take the trough of the wave?"
~ Anne Morrow Lindbergh*

Stand Back

There is so much to fear
in the course of a day.

What you thought was an errant poppy seed
has a death grip on your ankle.
Laptop anti-virus warnings are
leaking onto your fingertips.
There are carpenter ants in the attic,
mold in the basement,
lock-downs in the elementary school.
Blackbirds rain down from the mid-western sky.

You dream of cholera.

Even at Shop and Save,
lingering among the leeks, cauliflower, and romaine
you hear the rumbling of thunder,
the crackle of lightning
and then a disembodied voice from
somewhere in the ceiling tiles:

> "*Produce misting is about to begin.
> Stand back.*"

And you do,
grateful for the warning,
because where else can you hear
with such clarity
how to behave in the face of the deluge.

Rivers Rising

You should know that we did not separate
when we were herded up that gangplank

two by two, then down below, decks smeared
inside and out with pitch on wood.

The Flood Hero was kindly towards us, and
after he quenched our thirst with beer and wine

from clay pots and filled our bellies with grain,
we lost fear of rivers rising, battened

down ears to ravens' cries strangled by wind:
do not abandon us, do not aband...

Rumps, hocks, heads, hides, hooves, tails twitching,
estrus heating dank air like mystery.

We did not separate, we broke the Rules,
beastly desires, perhaps the last coupling—

moans, bellows, flank to thurl before the threat
of drowning hurly burly into night.

The Crossing
> *"this thing of darkness/ I*
> *Acknowledge mine." Prospero, The Tempest*

                     E-e-e-e cried the hungry babe,
               Cree-e-e wailed the wheeling saviour birds.
See how pink he is, they marveled—
as sweet as a scallop,
his eyes pieces of sky.

I am drawn to such tales:
"St.Kenneth and the Gulls"
who found him floating
in a basket on the Bristol Channel.

Is this what it takes to be loved?
To be a wild-child sailor
without words or compass,
bereft of motherlove and mothernest

only a few days old   abandoned

by his Welsh father-prince,
who knows why.

Did you see my infant face in your face?
Did you not hear my howls?

They carried him to their cliffside colony,
pulled downy feathers from their
own breasts for a nest.

Father, where were you
during my rough channel crossing?

No cold stones for this orphan.
He grew strong and kind and joyful
happy to share in mercy
as it moved throughout the world,
revered by the local peasants.

A forest doe came every morning
to feed him with her milk.
An angel offered a cup.

Sometimes

I like to imagine
I'm Mary Shelley's mother and
she is seven. We are walking on
Race Point Beach, fingers intertwined.

She is wearing a two-piece spandex suit
from H&M, Van Gogh yellow. I coat
her pale British skin with SPF 80,
"dermatologist recommended."

She is learning to swim in the
soft Atlantic surf, not that dreary
Lake Geneva where it always rains and
Mont Blanc casts shadows like male totems.

In this light   she is a minnow—
silver, streaming her way into the shoals,
her breath not shallow, but buoyant.
She surfaces.

"Well done, Mary, well done!" I cry.
Common Terns soar and screech
their choral validation, their creature
eyes green, glowing like small fires.

I swaddle her in a blue-striped towel
warmed by the June sun. We huddle
together and laugh at nothing and at
everything. What do I wish for her?

That her longing to be loved
has ebbed. I kiss each new freckle
splashed across her nose. She smiles
and licks salt off my shoulder.

Nocturne, in Red and Black

Tonight, twilight
   I spot paw prints

on the roof of
   my neighbor's truck—

a fox, likely,
   out foraging for

mice, squirrels, sand crabs
   for three pups burrowed

under an abandoned
   porch, barking their

hopes and hungers
   a cappella under

April stars, dogwood
   scenting the air. Imagine

the vixen returning
   mouth full, her red-

gold coat lustrous, slick
   from rain, her forelegs

gloved in sleek black like
   the arms of one of Whistler's

society darlings during
   a night of dancing, children

awaiting her arrival home, eager
   too for tokens of maternal bounty

not unlike this fish head,
   this spine, this blood,

briny matter before sleep—
   a feeding fervent, feral.

Minor Deviations

I want to love you, pi, or at least admire you,
in part to appease my husband who
is never happier than when talking about

irrational numbers, repetition and random distribution.
"Pi is *transcendental*," he pleads. But today alone
there's so much else competing for my devotion:

the Carolina Wren nesting in a blue shirt pocket
drying on the clothes line, singing her descending
triplet *"tea kettle, tea kettle, tea kettle,"*

the fog horn at Long Point streaming
a perfect A-flat out to sea—
the night awash in gray and ochre,

the thought of William Blake, who
at the age of four, believed he saw the face
of God pressed against his window pane.

What We Know

He recites prime numbers
when anxious like when he hears
the electric toothbrush, TV laugh tracks
                        23571113171923293137...
until I ask *What does 31 look like?*
Sometimes he'll find the crayon,
always burnt sienna, and draws
what looks like roasted garbanzo beans.
So how about 103? his dad will ask.
And always the same—
a canvas of circles. Pennies?
Six-year-old-boy-code for *GET ME OUT OF HERE?*
                        23571113171923293137...

When the light is right, slanting in
from the northern window, I envision
Seurat's paintings, those lovely French
coastal towns, thousands of jewel-like dots
where a vast sky meets a tranquil sea
at the horizon and think
some day I'll take my son to MoMA—
floor after floor of cadmium yellow,
fuchsia, cerulean,   ceilings without end.

But now it's 10:45—
the routine of the fish bowl
that I lift carefully from atop the fridge.
I remove his helmet,
covered in Ninja Warrior de-cals.
Nathaniel lets me rest both hands,
lightly, on his shoulders, as he watches
the Fantail and Bubble Eye swim
round and round and round
in their silent world, a world
with no sharp edges, his small face
pressed against the glass looking in.

Argonauta

"Ceviche," you say
as we sit in a small cafe
in Oaxaca, your first trip
out of the country.
"I'll have the ceviche."

My young daughter,
shimmering like a daystar
telling the waiter what
she'd like for lunch,
and, "*por favor*, some melon water."

And it's then I know
there are worlds you'll go
to when I'm not ready,
your mouth unmoored and hungry
for life raw and briny below,

like the paper nautilus, not
fastened to her shell at all,
a mere cradle for the eggs,
a temporary dwelling
before the young sail away.

As if the sea can offer everything.
As if the sea were the only life-bearer.

Departures

Your Lufthansa flight leaves in
twenty minutes for Madrid where
you will read Literatura and
Historia y Arte for three months

without your mother who is not taking
this at all well: the cloying smells
from Cinnabon make my teeth ache.
My IBS has flared up. I've lost my Smartphone.

You are nineteen and have dreamt about
the Museo Reina Sofia, The Prado, Valencia
oranges juice-luscious, and clubbing with
slim-hipped young men named Mateo and Rafael.

I want to be the Dalai Lama who
as small child would ride on
his mother's back when she picked
barley and chilies in Amdo; he would

pull her left ear when he wanted to go
left, the other to go right, as I would
direct your path when you stroll the
Plaza Mayor looking only straight ahead.

Metamorphosis

Act I

From a distance they looked like
two Glad trash bags
billowing in the April dusk,
a plastic adagio.
But when I walked closer
I could see

Act II

those small turkey heads,
long, fan-shaped tails,
glossy, bronze wings dragging,
dark, rufous, feathery tips,
a prince-like display, the male
strutting his comic brio,
wattles ablaze like pieces of the heart,
an offering.

And the hen, dreaming of poults,
yelping in response to the call
of her polygamous lover,
a sudden ballon skyward on her
scrawny legs before the
destined coupling.

Act III

No evil sorcerer,
no promise of fidelity,
no Lake of Tears—
instead a grayblack disappearing act
into open fields,
all eyes on the roost,
stage left.

Fifteen

After baseball practice you'd bike to our place
behind the red barn, behind hay bales.
We'd kiss for hours until our lips ached and
blistered purple—battered boats on rocky shores.

We were a rain forest of desire. Your face
tasted of sweat and peaches, your
mouth French fries and Gatorade—
a wormhole into another universe.

The Beach Boys pulsed from a transistor
radio stuffed into my back pocket of
white denim shorts: *Oom bop bop*
good vibration, oom bop bop...

Such sweetness could make a small god jealous.
Who hasn't longed for that kind of love?

Flying Light

When we wake to find we are alone,
when the time comes when we can
no longer say we're sorry, when
a scree of regrets ascends into clarity
at the edge of the garden wall—
when can we ask the heart

to rise again, to recall women wending
their way to the stone well, that young
boy diving off the wharf at dusk—
cadences of light splashing skyward,
the hummingbird hovering for sugar
water in your rough, cupped hand,

the way heat always gravitates to cold.

Arrhythmia

> *But I will wear my heart on my sleeve for daws*
> *to peck at. ~Othello*

Just for today will you wear
your heart on your sleeve?
The crows, sated, have
retreated to their roosts.

Those words you swallowed last night
over risotto and recriminations
suggest a heart on attack.

Hand me saw and scalpel
to slice out that four-chambered,
hollow organ hidden
beneath a coterie of artery and

I'll suture it to your left arm,
warmed in gray flannel
leaving your right one free

to walk the dog, like you promised,
before night falls and it
starts to snow.
Doppler Radar predicts

below normal temperatures
and a high pressure system
fast approaching.

Derma Blues

These days I'm sure envying
the wood frog.
She can loosen her old skin,
twist her froggy body all around
and pull it over her froggy head
like a worn out sweater. Then
she eats it, leaving no trace of
her former self, *transformed.*

Mine, on the other hand, is
bruised, burned, Botoxed-
rosacea stippling my facial canvas,
cellulite cratering each thigh,
a bleedinghearttattoo
humiliating my left humerus.

And sometimes, in my dreams,
skin like alabaster, I'm still
waiting for that grim frog prince
to eat off the golden plate,
to sleep on my satin pillow
for three nights, and
croon, like Van Morrison,

> *"Princess darling, please
> let me love you."*

Solace at the P.O.

So, it's my turn and I place an envelope
on the counter. The clerk asks:

"Does this package contain any hazardous liquid?"
Only a thousand tears, I reply.

Is there anything flammable or breakable?"
Just my heart, I say.

"Would you like this sent express mail
for an additional $7.50?"
Actually, I'd prefer a slow delivery,
maybe in a canvas saddlebag, on a
dappled mare, rambling through mountains,
through valleys lush and deep, pausing
for long drinks in stony creeks.

How about insurance?"
We both know there's no insurance,
no deductible, for matters like this;
I know what I have given,
what I have received.

He glances at the customer line lengthening—
impatience spreading like a virus.

I want him to close his window and ask me
to meet him out back. He'll be wearing cowboy
boots and smell like fresh cut locust burl.

He'll drape his tattooed arm (wild boar)
around me, offer a cigarette and say
"A dog walks into a bar..."

Alchemy

My daughter and I dropped by
for sweet corn at Quincy's Farm and
fed some tender husks to the donkey
through a crack in the white fence.

She stroked his hairy cheeks, and
festooned his head with the silk.
He nudged her for a good scratch
while he chewed, his teeth
like decaying marble pillars.

Suddenly, he tossed his head back,
tilted his ears, his eyes dazed
as if awakened from
a midsummer's dream,
and brayed like a symphonic horn
section warming up, F-sharp minors
ricocheting off the red barn.

"He knows Mr.Quincy's coming in his truck,"
the farmer's wife said. "We think
he smells the diesel."

No magic potion from
Cupid's misfed arrow,
no Fairy Queen betrayed
by her petty husband-king, only

Tom, weary and stooped
after a long day in a hot field,
an unlikely lover, but a conjurer
of sorts, offering a bucket of water,
maybe some sweet oats for supper,

trailing tiny particles of exhaust,
a toxin, that can fill
our lungs and hearts
as sometimes love can.

Reverie, Morning

The next time you start
the coffee grinder
at 4:00 a.m.
on Saturday
in February
because you couldn't sleep,
I will try to imagine you
as a pileated woodpecker
drumming on the near dead
oak by the frozen patio,
defending our territory,
our nest, or even better
tapping a courtship call
to me huddled under our
blue, down comforter, hungry
for the suet and raw peanuts
you hung on the Foil-a-Squirrel
feeder—your red fishing cap
a flare in the pre-dawn hours.

Here on Earth
> *Your Horoscope Today by Marlene*
> *"Tonight: You know what to do."*

I'm not sure I do, Marlene,
because before he
left for work today

we argued whether it was
Etta or Ella who sang
"You will find you were blind,"

and if glucosamine really
strengthens cartilage. Well, I said,
Luna gulps down her canine capsule

cloaked in ground round and
bounds her way into the
daggers of the February night

without that St. Sebastian
tied-to-the-post-martyrdom-look
you got from your mother who

still mispronounces my name
after what seems like twenty years
of speaking in tongues. And

last night you asked if
I knew how to convert
inches into pixels. Who cares,

said I, dreaming instead of
this celestial sphere and
how to sail across the seas

every orphaned child to rooms
spare now of grown daughters'
beating hearts and breathing lungs.

But before the sun disappears
behind the wrack line of
another day of mystery,

I'll try to silence this moral nebulae
on my lower astral shelf and
 find, instead, thyme for the

roast chicken we'll eat for dinner
and wait for the stars to stretch
across the evening sky.

Sky Watch
> *Everything changes, nothing is lost.*
> *~Ovid*

Mostly they're damn annoying,
these gray, black specks and strings
floating in my left eye,
        clumpingandcoating—
shadows on the retina.

But sometimes, after moonset,
when city lights obscure
Cassiopeia's topsy-turvy throne,
I recall the time you said,
light-years ago,
as our own, young planet
seemed to orbit the sun,
and the pull of love
was too strong to defy:

> *"On a dark, summer night*
>   *you can see five thousand stars."*

And then those microscopic fibers
become
        a   milky   blaze   of
            meteors   streaking   across
    my own November sky

       gas   *light*   *dust*

for Dorothy Wordsworth

Some say she led a half life—
motherless at six,
fatherless at twelve,
separated from her brothers
for twenty years
especially William, her favorite.

Together they wandered Grasmere,
not lonely, up the purple crag
across the turf,
fairy valleys in the vale,
Primroses by the roadside,
Pile worts that shone like stars of gold
in the Sun,
she wrote,
he the Poet, she the secretary.
"Unlady-like behaviour"
decried a great aunt,
all that walking.
Then over and over again
returning home
to make the tea,
to make the porridge,
to feed the beggars at the cottage door.
Overworked, underpaid, no health care.

What makes a life whole?

No image of her exists in that world,
only one near the invalid-end—
plump, toothless, still *wild-eyed*,
wrote William.

Early Warning Signs

They mock her at the Quench water cooler;
they call her "Gamma Ray Girl" even though
she's the other side of sixty. She says
she's survived spontaneous combustion.

"Imagine," she whispers, a voice wizened
from lack of use: "compost, vapor spiraling
from a hay stack's surface, acrid tobacco
smell, pistachios bursting from their bins."

I tend to believe her—maybe it's the
scars like pink ribbons rippling above her
breastbone. It can grow cold around the heart;
sometimes we need to self-heat, to embrace
the thermal runaway and then ignite.

When charred torsos are found, she says, there is
usually little sign of struggle.

Musa Nana

You know what March can do, only nudging
into spring, with a paltry gift of noon
sun. She lures you onto the sidewalk clean
of snow but for a slice of ice, enough
to catapult you into the shrubs. Winds
like furies assail you for crimes unspoken,
gutter muck, frozen, backed up to heaven;
mourning doves struggle to find their songs.

But then you're in Star Market; a herald,
a little like Gabriel himself, arms
like angel wings, cloaked in gray fleece
announces: "*The bananas have arrived.*"
And on this day that you thought was barren
behold—Oahu-warm, a kind of grace.

Sappho Sings to the Syrian Migrants on Lesbos

"We have run from war," a father cries.
        Across the salt sea, the rose-fingered moon.

"We are hungry and thirsty,"
        And in my wild heart what I most wish—

He jumps into shallow water, stumbling on rocks.
        With pain and sorrow—In pity come

a young couple who smirk and take a selfie.
        Some say a fleet of ships is the loveliest sight-

A mother, her scarf streaked with salt, her infant lifeless, wails.
        Help, oh help, quickly send relief.

They search for shade and shelter: Roses and
        tender thyme and the blooming honey-lotus

before the trek through mountains to Mytilene Port
        And suffer not my heart to break with grief.

When a Black Bear Came to Truro

I like to think of him swimming the Canal
unnoticed, against the current, against
credulity, legs stronger than any freestyler,
a dark shadow in salt water and then
lumbering his maleness, his aloneness
north on 6A to Ballston Beach.
"It was a black bear, all right—
sure as you were born," said Tommy Dyer,
a fisherman on The Little Eva.

I like to think of him, scratching his back on
pitch pines, leaving scat in his wake:
grubs, apples, seeds—steam rising like a signal,
and him mumbling, squeaking, panting—
a scent of a young sow perhaps, a scent of
Wampanoag fires, of ancient deer bones,
swales of genetic memory guiding him
back home under a purple sky—part
healer, part magician that was bear.

More than we ask for, more than we need

Each night from the treetops,
from our murderous roost,
we watch you set out a tray of
kibble, chicken skin, baby carrots
for us
        quaquaqua

for you,
tomorrow, we will leave a
key, a kite string, a crocus bulb
and recall the time you placed
a green avocado on the

glass table to ripen in the sun—
your hair like black silk

        quaquaqua

Sandy Longley lives in Delmar, NY and spends summers in Provincetown, MA surrounded by the Atlantic Ocean and Cape Cod Bay. The Outer Cape Artist in Residence Consortium recently awarded her a two-week stay to live and write in the solitude of the dunes. She is an Associate Professor of English at Columbia-Greene Community College in Hudson, NY. In 2012 and 2015 she was shortlisted for Dorset's Bridport Prize.

www.ingramcontent.com/pod-product-compliance
Lightning Source LLC
LaVergne TN
LVHW041507070426
835507LV00012B/1393